Seals and Sea Lions

DAVID GEORGE GORDON

MONTEREY BAY AQUARIUM®

Monterey, California

The purpose of the Monterey Bay Aquarium is to stimulate interest, increase knowledge and promote stewardship of Monterey Bay and the world's ocean environment through innovative exhibits, public education and scientific research.

Acknowledgments This book draws heavily on the work of many marine scientists who kindly shared their information on pinnipeds with me. I thank them for their generosity and guidance. In particular, I thank Marianne Riedman, Jim Harvey and Steven Webster for their thorough review of the manuscript. I am also grateful to Nora Deans, Lisa Tooker, Roxane Buck, Eileen Campbell, Natasha Fraley and James Stockton for their roles in transforming the text. I thank field biologist and author Victor Scheffer for inspiring and encouraging me.

Published in the United States by the Monterey Bay Aquarium Foundation, 886 Cannery Row, Monterey, CA 93940–1085.

Library of Congress Cataloging in Publication Data:

Gordon, David G. (David George), 1950–
Seals and sea lions / by David George Gordon.
p. cm.
Includes index.
ISBN 1-878244-06-X
1. Pinnipedia. I. Title.
QL737.P6G67 1994
599.74'5—dc20   94-39725 CIP

Photo and Illustration Credits:

Cover: Dugald Stermer
Back Cover: Lanting, Frans/Minden Pictures
Arctic Studies Center, Smithsonian Institution: 52 (bottom), 54
Balthis, Frank S.: 23 (bottom), 27 (top), 28 (bottom), 30 (top), 45, 57, 58 (top), 60
Braud, Dominique/Tom Stack & Assoc.: 56
Bucich, Richard A.: 11 (top), 32 (bottom), 33 (top)
Chamberlain, Marc C.: 9 (top inset), 49, 50
Conlin, Mark: 16, 61 (bottom)

Courtesy of Bert Kellogg Collection of the North Olympic Library System Port Angeles, WA: 52 (top)
©Curtsinger, Bill: 44, 46, 62
Davis, Chuck: 40–41
Davis, John: 51
Ellis, Gerry: 12, 32 (top), 37, 39, 53 (top inset), 59
Foott, Jeff: 7, 11 (bottom), 13, 15, 17, 21, 28 (top), 30 (bottom), 31, 34–35, 47, 53, 61 (top)
Foott, Jeff/Tom Stack & Assoc.: 4
Hall, Howard/HHP: 36
Herrmann, Richard: 9 (middle inset), 38, 42 (top)

Johnson, Mike: 10, 33 (bottom), 58 (bottom)
Johnson, Thomas M./ Earthviews: 26–27, 29
Kitchin, Thomas/Tom Stack & Assoc.: 24–25
Lanting, Frans/Minden Pictures: 6, 18
Leatherwood, Stephen/ Earthviews: 1, 19
Roessler, Carl: 42 (bottom)
Shaw, John/Tom Stack & Assoc.: 55
Snyderman, Marty: 14, 43
Todd, Frank S./Earthviews: 53 (bottom inset)
Tyler, Diana Dee: 63
Westmorland, F. Stuart: 9, 20, 23 (top), 48

Series & Book Editor : Nora L. Deans
Designer : James Stockton, James Stockton & Associates
Composition : Wilsted & Taylor
Printed in Hong Kong through Global Interprint, Santa Rosa, CA, USA

CONTENTS

A sea lion glides in silence through the darkness, 600 feet beneath the storm-tossed surface of the sea. At this depth, the water may be calm, but the pressure is extreme. At more than 260 pounds per square inch, it could easily crush the chest of any human swimmer.

In these cold, dark and demanding surroundings, the sea lion is at ease. It can remain submerged for many minutes, return to the surface for a breath of fresh air, then effortlessly descend.

Below the waves, the sea lion won't suffer for lack of food or companionship. The ocean offers a variety of foods to choose from and several other sea lions are nearby. Well fed and wrapped in warm layers of insulating fat, the sea lions can forage at sea as long as they choose. Later they'll return to shore to bask in the sun and nap on the rocks.

The sea lion, like every other species of seal and sea lion, is superbly adapted to many of life's challenges on land and at sea. Yet only now, after decades of land-based observation and commercial pursuit, are we in a position to more fully understand these marine mammals and their lives along our coastlines and far below the waves.

It's difficult to generalize about all seals and sea lions. Each pinniped species is unique, and even among groups like northern fur seals there are enough variations to invalidate nearly every sweeping statement about life histories, feeding and breeding strategies or behaviors.

In the following pages, you'll read about the adaptations and endurance of many pinnipeds with particular focus on five species— California sea lions, Steller sea lions, northern elephant seals, northern fur seals and harbor seals. All illustrate important facets of pinniped life and each can be observed with relative ease, from a boat or on shore, in North American seas.

1

PINNIPEDS

Throughout history, few animals have meant so much to so many different people as the pinnipeds—the warm-blooded, flipper-footed inhabitants of the world's oceans. To many people living or visiting along rocky ocean coasts, seals and sea lions are sources of wonderment. To others, they are sources of food. Fishermen and other folks who make their living from the sea may regard them as nuisances, the voracious marauders of commercial fish traps and nets. Throughout the nineteenth century, when fur seal coats and hats were all the fashion, pinnipeds' pelts fueled the lucrative fur trade.

Despite our long association with seals and sea lions, we knew relatively little about their private lives until recently. Now, with current technologies, we can peer into the pinnipeds' world, which, in some cases, is more than a hundred miles from shore and nearly one mile below the sea.

Every year, marine labs and field stations from Mexico to the Aleutian Islands of Alaska collect new information about pinnipeds. Our old ideas about seals and sea lions are rapidly being discarded as we learn more about their lives at sea.

PINNIPEDS: A CURIOUS, QUARRELSOME TRIBE To eighteenth-century scientist Carolus Linnaeus, seals and sea lions were "A dirty, curious, quarrelsome tribe, easily tamed and polygamous." In his efforts to classify all living things, Linnaeus placed these animals in the order *Pinnipedia*, a name that combined two Latin words—*pinna*, meaning fin, wing or feather and *pedis*, meaning foot. He called the animals in this order the pinnipeds, and wrote that "they inhabit and swim under water and crawl on land with difficulty because of their retracted fore-feet and united hind-feet."

His was a good choice of names for these creatures with wing-like feet. Called flippers, the dramatically modified limbs of seals and sea lions serve both as paddles and as rudders, enabling pinnipeds to swim and dive with great speed and agility.

Besides flippers, the 33 living species of pinnipeds share several other distinctive physical traits. They are all mammals, with body temperatures that stay more or less stable throughout their lives. Their streamlined, torpedo-shaped bodies are wrapped in thick layers of fat. And most members of this clan have large eyes, slit-like nostrils that can open and shut, prominent muzzles and pointed, conical teeth.

These adaptations serve pinnipeds well in the ocean and only

All pinnipeds, including this young northern elephant seal (below) and California sea lions (right), have distinctive faces and flipper feet.

slightly less well on land. Unlike whales and dolphins, which live their entire lives at sea, pinnipeds divide their time to varying degrees between water and land. In this respect they are amphibious animals—comfortable with spending weeks, even months far out at sea, yet periodically returning to land to rest, mate and rear young. Many pinnipeds live this nomadic lifestyle in a gregarious manner, gathering to breed in large groups called colonies or rookeries.

Today, some scientists have challenged Linnaeus' placement of pinnipeds in an order all to themselves. They divide living pinnipeds and their precursors among three families of the *Carnivora*, an order that includes the families of bears, cats, dogs and several other land-dwelling mammals. But scientists on both sides of the debate agree that there are three distinct pinniped families—earless seals (Phocidae), eared seals (Otariidae) and walruses (Odobenidae).

EARLESS SEALS: THE PHOCIDS Members of the pinniped family Phocidae are often called earless seals in reference to the absence of ear flaps (or pinnae) among this bunch. Although lacking these flaps, the phocids do, in fact, have ears—small openings that lead to the ear canal—behind their eyes.

Eighteen species of phocids, including the harp seal (*Phoca groenlandica*), Weddell seal (*Leptonychotes weddelli*) and endangered Hawaiian monk seal (*Monachus schauinslandi*), can be found in the world's oceans. Two phocid species—the harbor seal (*Phoca vitulina*) and northern elephant seal (*Mirounga angustirostris*)—are regularly seen along the Pacific coast of the United States.

The flippers of phocids are easily distinguished from those of other pinnipeds. Short fore flippers have a claw on each of five digits. Hind flippers are also clawed, with a thin webbing of skin connecting the digits. Phocids can flex the digits on both fore and hind flippers while grooming themselves, or when clinging to slippery rock faces or hauling themselves out of the water and onto ice floes.

A phocid's hind flippers angle towards its rear, and cannot be rotated forward. To move across dry land, phocids must balance their weight on their staunch fore flippers and wriggle and bounce along on their bellies.

While disadvantaged on land, phocids move swiftly through the water. Flattened fore flippers serve as rudders for steering while hind flippers are for stroking, providing the animal with plenty of thrust. Stroking combined with the shimmying side-to-side movements of their muscular bodies moves many members of this family at peak speeds of 14 to 24 miles per hour.

One of 18 phocid species, the harbor seal (right) lacks ear flaps. Digits on its short fore flippers are tipped with sharp claws, used for grooming or grabbing hold of ice floes and rocks.

THE SECRET LANGUAGE OF SEALS AND SEA LIONS

"Hey! Hello there." When Hoover the harbor seal spoke these words, the entire staff of the New England Aquarium stopped to listen. A popular attraction on the Boston harborfront for several years, Hoover had evidently learned how to produce sounds that resemble human speech, perhaps mimicking the voices of attendants or people passing by along the waterfront.

Male harbor seals may learn to vocalize by imitating other male seals. It's possible that Hoover picked up his human-like vocal sounds from his keepers at an early age.

Hoover's skill as a mimic points to pinnipeds' astounding capacity for making vocal sounds. Barks, clicks, squeals and other sounds serve a multitude of purposes—both above and below the water.

Underwater, some phocids produce a wide range of sounds that may be useful for maintaining territories, keeping in touch with pups and others of their kind. Weddell seals and a few other polar species appear to have the largest repertoire of underwater sounds, which they use with the greatest frequency. It's been suggested that the clicking noises made by these animals are for echolocation, guiding them through murky water or to breathing holes in the ice. The evidence to support this assertion has yet to be obtained.

Otariids are fairly quiet in water but quite

loud on land. Their ringing vocalizations sound out battle cries or warning calls to territorial rivals. Some species tend to broadcast sounds in all directions. Others aim calls at specific animals. The male northern elephant seal's large, fleshy proboscis channels and amplifies sound much like a trumpet's brass coils, adding extra resonance to already loud sounds. Head thrown back, the elephant seal directs its vocal blasts at particular opponents more than 50 yards away.

Threat vocalizations of male elephant seals may differ from one breeding colony to the next, suggesting that some species of pinnipeds vocalize in regional dialects.

Such dialects are also found in Weddell seals and bearded seals (*Erignathus barbatus*). While it is unclear how they originated and how they are maintained, seal dialects may help scientists track the movements of pinniped populations over time.

Most pinniped mothers and their pups keep in touch by making their own distinctive calls. In otariids, each pup's call is different from any other—perhaps the only way that a mother can find her young on a crowded beach. Otariid mothers also emit special calls when returning from feeding trips at sea. Should more than one pup respond to her call, the mother picks out her own offspring's voice from the din.

A California sea lion vocalizes under water, producing a barrage of bubbles (left). The roar of an adult northern elephant seal (right) and the high-pitched cry of a weaned elephant seal pup (below) are other ways that pinnipeds communicate.

EARED PINNIPEDS: THE OTARIIDAE Within the pinniped family Otariidae, ear holes are covered by external flaps, a characteristic that gives rise to their common name—eared seals. Represented by five species of sea lions and nine species of fur seals, the otariids live primarily in the Pacific Ocean and along its coast. Only three otariid species make their homes in North American waters—the Steller sea lion (*Eumetopias jubatus*), California sea lion (*Zalophus californianus*), and northern fur seal (*Callorhinus ursinus*). A fourth, the Guadalupe fur seal (*Arctocephalus townsendi*), is an occasional visitor to the southern California coast.

Otariids have somewhat longer necks than phocids. Their fore flippers are only partially haired. The first digits are longer and larger than the rest. Hind flippers are more flexible than those of a phocid. They rotate forward, beneath the body, making movement on land less of a chore. In water, otariids can practically fly, using their paddle-shaped fore flippers to reach comfortable swimming speeds of 18 miles per hour—nearly eight times the speed of most human swimmers. In short bursts, eared seals are almost twice this fast.

From a distance, it can be difficult to tell sea lions apart from fur seals. The most recognizable difference is the fur seal's thick, double-layer coat. A short, dense underfur surrounds long individual guard hair—resulting in a coat that was prized by hunters in the eighteenth, nineteenth and twentieth centuries. Also, fur seals' snouts come to more of a point than the broader, blunted noses of most sea lions.

Otariids, including South American fur seals (below) and Stellar sea lions (right), have obvious ear flaps and flexible hind flippers.

FOOD AND FORAGING

Where the fishing is best, California sea lions congregate.

"If it moves, we eat it" could very well be the motto of the pinniped clan, whose members consume nearly every major form of life, excluding plants, in the sea. Many pinnipeds eat fish, shrimp and squids. Others devour penguins and other marine birds. Still others dine on shellfish or capture tiny shrimp-like krill and other small, swarming organisms in the sea. A few, including the walrus and leopard seals, even eat other seals and sea lions. Even more exotic fare has been discovered in the stomachs of leopard seals, whose diet in southern Australian waters apparently includes an occasional platypus or poisonous sea snake.

The diets of individual species can vary with the season and availability of food, especially for those seals that live in polar- and subpolar environments. For many pinnipeds, diets also change over the course of a lifetime. Newly weaned harp seals, for example, feed on zooplankton—tiny free-swimming animals—near the surface of the water. However, as they grow older, they start to capitalize on the abundance of schooling capelin fish at intermediate depths. As adults, they can dive even deeper, filling their stomachs with bottom-dwelling fish and crustaceans.

Pinnipeds seeking food on the move must expend lots of energy to capture prey. Cooperative foraging strategies often prove useful, especially when large schools of fish or squids are around. Ordinarily solitary foragers, California sea lions and several other otariid species come together to capitalize on such abundances of prey. In large groups, they can actually herd schooling fish into tight formations, making it easier for the pinnipeds to pick off several fish with one pass-through. California sea lions have been observed feeding cooperatively with harbor porpoises (*Phocoena phocoena*) in Monterey Bay.

Many pinnipeds swallow stones. We're not sure why they do this, but it's been suggested that this may help with digestion or somehow aid in buoyancy or balance. Some scientists think seals eat stones to fill their stomachs during breeding or molting seasons—typically times when they forgo food. In some cases, the quantity of stones in a pinniped's belly is extreme: a single southern sea lion (*Otaria byronia*) reportedly carried 77 pounds of such ballast without difficulty.

Although several otariids drink sea water (and Weddell seals may even eat snow on occasion), most pinnipeds obtain the water they need from the digestion of prey, or, while fasting, from the metabolism of blubber. Studies of harbor seals show that these animals get 90 percent of their fresh water from the fish they eat.

WHAT ABOUT WALRUSES? The third pinniped family, Odobenidae, contains only one living species, the walrus (*Odobenus rosmarus*). Its substantial bulk (males can weigh as much as 3,400 pounds) and distinctive pair of canine teeth, called tusks, make this resident of frigid Arctic seas hard to mistake for any other marine mammal. The scientific name of this genus means "tooth-walker," an allusion to the walrus' ability to use its tusks as pick axes with which to haul itself from the water. Among males, these tusks can also be used as weapons in territorial battles with other walruses.

Like phocids, walruses lack ear flaps. However, like otariids, they can turn their hind flippers to amble about on land. Many scientists consider walruses to be evolutionary intermediates between the other two pinniped families.

Remains of ancient walrus ancestors indicate this enigmatic family evolved from a sea lion-like forebear, at least 22 million years ago. In the Pacific, fossilized walrus bones and tusks have been found on the coast of Mexico and, in the Atlantic, as far south as Florida. Today, however, these animals live only in arctic and subarctic climates. Along the west coast of North America, they rarely venture south of the Bering Sea.

Sharp tusks become weapons in territorial disputes among male walruses. At other times, walruses use their canine teeth as pick axes to haul themselves from the water onto ice flows.

ADAPTATIONS OF WORLD CHAMPION SWIMMERS Seals, sea lions and walruses—while distinctly adapted to their particular lifestyles—share certain attributes common to all pinnipeds. While some species are more adept than others at swimming, diving or walking, all have undergone adaptive changes enabling them to excel under conditions that, to most land animals, would be deemed inhospitable at best.

In the cold Pacific, thick fur may not keep an animal warm for long periods—and several pinniped species lack thick fur. While swimming and diving, most pinnipeds rely on their layers of blubber to maintain their body temperatures, which may be as much as 60 degrees Fahrenheit higher than the surrounding seas. An all-encompassing jacket of fat, called blubber, can be several inches thick in some species and ensures that the seal or sea lion will stay warm even in the coldest climes. Most pinniped pups are born with very little blubber, but within weeks develop their own fatty jackets. The dense coats of northern fur seals help augment the insulating properties of blubber.

A pinniped's large, highly sensitive eyes help it peer through the murk of coastal seas. Whether these animals depend on their hearing to navigate and find food is a subject of debate among scientists.

Most pinnipeds have a weak sense of smell. As for touch, the sensitive mustache-like whiskers (known as vibrissae) play an important role in many species. These bristles may contain ten times more nerve fibers than are typically found in a land animal's whiskers. Their increased sensitivity helps pinnipeds search for food in dark, deep waters and may even serve as navigational aids, helping seals to locate the centers of breathing holes in the ice.

Cumbersome on land, a harbor seal maneuvers with grace and agility through the murky ocean depths.

To hunt for food at great depths, a pinniped must hold its breath under extreme pressure for long periods. The world champion for such breath-hold dives is the northern elephant seal, which can remain submerged for more than an hour while diving to depths of more than 4,000 feet. To accomplish such impressive diving feats, pinnipeds have evolved a blood supply that is proportionately much larger and more capable of absorbing and holding oxygen than most other mammals. While diving, a pinniped's heartbeat slows. Blood is shunted away from peripheral organs and directed to the brain, lungs and heart. Enlarged passageways in the skull deliver blood to the brain, supplying oxygen reserves to this vital nerve center.

A pinniped's teeth are also modified for life in the ocean. While many animals use their teeth to cut or chew food into smaller pieces, pinnipeds usually swallow smaller prey whole, rather than risk biting it into pieces that could float away. These animals' teeth are designed to catch and hold fish and other slippery sea life.

Many pinnipeds, like this sea lion, have pointed conical teeth for grasping slippery fish under water.

QUICK TO LEARN The ease with which captive seals and sea lions learn "tricks" seems to indicate a strong cognitive ability among pinnipeds. Yet such sideshow talents are shared by many animals, including dogs, elephants and parrots. Comparing the intelligence of one animal species to another is often a futile exercise because, simply put, every kind of animal is best at performing the specific tasks it needs to survive.

Laboratory and field studies of California sea lions have highlighted this species' learning abilities, including the comprehension of an artificial language. In one series of experiments at the University of California's Long Marine Lab in Santa Cruz, a female sea lion named Rocky learned to respond to a vocabulary of more than 20 hand gestures. It took Rocky about two and a half years to recognize these gestures. As of this writing, however, she can comprehend over 7,000 combinations of these hand signs, retrieving specific objects and carrying out even more detailed tasks from her trainers.

Other signs of pinniped intelligence include the ability of many species to migrate over vast distances, and such advanced activities as "play" among pups. By continuing to study seals and sea lions in laboratories and in the wild, we can gain deeper insights into their cognitive processes.

Young sea lions tussle on land and play tag under water, possibly preparing themselves through play for later challenges in life.

THE TRADEMARK PINNIPED: CALIFORNIA SEA LIONS When most people think of a pinniped, they picture the California sea lion—the most familiar member of this large and diverse group of animals.

For decades, these sleek brown otariids have been star attractions at circuses in Europe and the United States. Easily trained at an early age to perform simple tricks, they entertain visitors at zoos, aquariums and marine parks throughout the world. Females are smaller and less aggressive than males, making them the preferred pupils of most professional animal trainers.

The common name of this sea lion reflects its primary habitat—the coastal waters of California, usually within 10 miles of shore. More than 80,000 of these animals make their home along this stretch of the mainland coast. Adults migrate southward to breeding grounds in the Channel Islands and Mexico each spring, returning each fall to California, Oregon, Washington and British Columbia. Others occupy the Pacific coast of Mexico year-round. Although a subspecies of sea lion (*Z.c. japonicus*) once inhabited the coast of Japan, they were overhunted and nearly vanished from Asia in the mid-1900s. Today, small populations can be found near several Korean islands. Another subspecies, the Galápagos sea lion (*Z.c. wollebaeki*), inhabits the waters off the rugged Galápagos Islands.

Raucous, abundant and undeniably entertaining, California sea lions are often sensitive to human disturbance and will leap off rocks into the water when disturbed.

While many people are familiar with the California sea lion's land-based activities, it's at sea that these agile otariids show off their real abilities. They sometimes leap clear of the water—a behavior called porpoising—to pick up speed as they cruise along. Skilled surfers, California sea lions ride the crests of incoming waves. Inquisitive by nature, they are attracted to fishing boats and, occasionally, snorkelers and scuba divers.

Leaping clear of the water, this porpoising pinniped can reach peak speeds of 35 miles per hour.

The California sea lion's swimming skills and ability to perform on cue are giving marine mammal researchers the opportunity to study whales at sea. Scientists at California's Moss Landing Marine Laboratory and Long Marine Laboratory are teaching sea lions to follow whales in the open sea while wearing special harnesses mounted with video cameras. If all goes as planned, scientists will soon be able to observe natural behavior on videotape, without causing any disturbance to the whales.

ORIGINS OF PINNIPEDS "In the mythos of the folk who make their living from the sea, it is well known that hidden in the dark pools of the eyes of certain seals are spirits that call out to certain men," wrote Victor Scheffer, wildlife biologist and author of *The Year of the Seal*. "These seals, they say, are really fisherfolk who were caught in some act displeasing to the gods and were made to live in hairy skins forever after and to wander at the will of the winds and the tides." Occasionally, Scheffer added, by saving the life of a drowning sailor, one of these seals can be freed from such enslavement. Transformed into a beautiful maiden, it will marry the sailor and live the rest of its life on land.

Among the members of today's scientific community, the origins of pinnipeds are less clear. Some scientists maintain that all pinnipeds share a common ancestor—a bear-like carnivore that lived roughly 30 million years ago. Others suggest that otariids and phocids evolved from different ancestral stocks—the otariids from a bear-like ancestor and the phocids from an otter-like one. They also propose that the two groups arose in different seas. According to this theory, the first otariids appeared in the Pacific

Ocean about 25 million years ago, roughly 3 to 5 million years before the first phocids appeared in the Atlantic Ocean.

The results of recent genetic studies support the theory that both otariids and phocids share a common ancestor. In one study of pinniped origins conducted at the University of California at Berkeley, the molecular structure of two proteins—albumen and transferrin—from several species of mammals were compared. These proteins from pinnipeds proved more closely related to those of dog-like carnivores than to proteins from any other mammals. The study also showed that proteins of phocids and otariids are even more closely related to each other than to those of the dog-like carnivores. These findings were supported by studies of different animal proteins conducted by other scientists in Europe, giving strength to the argument that pinnipeds are dog-like carnivores rather than members of a separate order of mammals.

Still the debate over pinniped origins continues today, confirming the rather wry observation of one turn-of-the-century scientist, that "on no one family of mammals have more diversities of opinion been expressed, both in the descriptions of different authors and in those of the same author at different times."

What are the relationships among living pinnipeds and in which seas did their ancestors evolve? The answers to these questions are not easily found.

2

A SOCIAL ANIMAL

From out of the fog comes an unearthly chorus of growls, gurgles and dog-like barking. Next comes the strong odor of fish, wet fur and feces, carried across the water by the steady southeasterly breeze. Finally, the fog parts and the rookery comes into view—a small island off the coast of Alaska, its rocky beach nearly hidden by the large brown bodies of Steller sea lions.

Each spring, several thousand of these impressive animals nestle together, many females with a pup and a 50-pound yearling at their sides. On the outer fringe of this noisy, odoriferous breeding ground lurk several adult males, gigantic creatures with broad, barrel-shaped chests and box-like brown heads. They are the territorial males, each keeping close watch over as many as 30 females and their offspring.

Three months ago, this particular stretch of beach was almost deserted. Then, practically overnight, it filled with seal lions. By summer's end, both males and females will return to the water. They won't come ashore here again until the following spring.

LIFE ON LAND Many earless seals breed on ice masses, either attached to land (so-called "fast ice") or adrift at sea ("pack ice"). Because the pack ice seals must contend with the instabilities of moving and melting ice, both mating and rearing of young are hurried affairs, usually conducted singly or in small groups.

Many pinniped species, including all otariids, breed on land—often on offshore islands or remote coasts. Favored sites are usually far from human disturbance yet close to their food supplies in the ocean. Here, mating and rearing young for otariids become more leisurely pursuits than for their ice-breeding relatives.

With exceptions such as the crabeater seal (*Lobodon carcinophagus*), ringed seal (*Phoca hispida*), and several other phocids, adult male pinnipeds mate with more than one female. Through such a reproductive strategy, called polygyny, one male can impregnate many females in a single breeding season, thus passing his genetic material to the largest possible number of pups. Male pinnipeds are not involved in their young's upbringing so, from a reproductive standpoint, their time is best spent breeding with as many females as they can.

Among land-breeding otariids and a few phocids such as elephant seals, adult males outsize the females in both size and weight. Through this phenomenon (known as sexual dimorphism), males can more easily assert their dominance over their smaller

*Relationships among
many phocid mothers
and pups are shaped by
the instabilities of ice.
On land, Steller sea
lions (below) can
devote more time to
their young.*

mates. Their great size also serves to announce their breeding
superiority over younger, less hefty males in the area.

Otariids and many phocids mate, give birth and rear their
young at sites called rookeries. The word "rookery" may have
originated centuries ago to describe the noisy gathering places
of birds, such as the European rook. However, its use today for
describing the equally noisy breeding places of the "feather-footed"

seals and sea lions seems to be perfectly appropriate.

In Steller sea lion rookeries, the dominant males, called bulls, control the movements of adult females. Steller bulls amass a stockpile of females to have many mates with which to copulate. The basic strategy is straightforward: bulls appear at the rookery several days or weeks before the breeding females arrive, stake out territories on land, then try to mate with all females.

Steller sea lion rookeries can be crowded and noisy— with 2,000 or more animals sharing one stretch of shore.

ENDANGERED IN ALASKAN SEAS

Like the threatened spotted owl of Pacific Northwest forests, the Steller sea lion has been on a collision course with big business—in this instance, commercial fishing interests in Alaska—for the last 30 years.

Between 1960 and 1990, populations in the heart of the species' range (the central and western Gulf of Alaska and eastern and central Aleutian Islands) have dropped by more than 100,000 juveniles and adults. Observations at rookeries and haul-out sites reveal an overall decline of 78 percent from the late 1950s to the early1990s.

The reasons for this dramatic decline are not well understood. Many biologists point to competition between Steller sea lions and commercial fisheries in Alaska. Steller sea lions routinely eat herring, salmon and other commercially harvested seafood. Of particular importance is the walleye pollock (*Theragra chalcogramma*), commonly sold at fish markets as whitefish or cod. From the 1970s to the present, millions of tons of walleye pollock have been removed each year from the seas in which the sea lions feed.

Such heavy fishing of this species has had an effect on the fish stocks: the overall size of pollock has diminished by 30 percent, and entire populations have dwindled. Large-scale commercial fishing operations have hurt Steller sea lions in other ways. It's estimated that over 20,000 of these animals were accidentally caught and killed in the nets of foreign and joint-venture trawlers between 1966 and 1988.

A five-year study of the effects of commercial fishing on Steller sea lions was authorized by Congress in 1988. Commercial fishermen assisted in this study and also took steps to reduce the accidental capture of seals and sea lions in their nets.

During 1989, about 56,000 Steller sea lions were counted at haul-out sites throughout coastal Alaska and Russia. Assuming that at least a third of the sea lions were away from the rookeries and haul-out sites at the time of the counts, the

population may have included no fewer than 75,000 animals—less than half their historic abundance on both sides of the Pacific Ocean.

In 1990, the National Marine Fisheries Service published an emergency rule, listing the Steller sea lion as a threatened species under the provisions of the Marine Mammal Protection Act. Other efforts to protect the remaining populations have been launched, including the halt of timber harvests (which can disturb the animals and degrade their coastal habitats) on at

least one of the important sea lion islands in the Gulf of Alaska.

"Overall, it is not clear what factors have contributed to the Steller sea lion population decline," concluded one recent status report, prepared by the Washington Department of Wildlife, adding that "a great deal of information vital to the effective management of the species is lacking. In spite of these information voids, there is an urgent need to take immediate actions to safeguard against further population declines, and to provide for their recovery."

Alaskan populations of Steller sea lions have declined drastically over the last three decades.

THE BURDEN OF BULLS It sounds simple, but in actual practice, defending territories is hard work. With loud barks and bold body language, bulls warn other males to stay clear of their territorial claims. If another bull tries to invade this space, battles may erupt. Actual physical contact between two bulls is often brief, preceded by much lengthier bouts of posturing and noise-making.

A bull's size and age usually determines the extent of his territory and the number of consecutive seasons that he will occupy it. In a study of Steller sea lion rookeries in the western Gulf of Alaska, 90 percent of the territories were held by bulls at their sexual peak, between nine and 13 years of age.

The most competitive bulls hold territories with the highest "real estate" values—determined by the general location, including access to water and the number of females that each territory contains. Steller sea lion bulls typically maintain their territories for two or three breeding seasons, although the same spot in a rookery may be held for up to seven consecutive seasons. Younger males and those lacking strength to stake such solid claims frequently occupy sites (called haul-out areas) neighboring the rookery grounds, sharing their turf with barren cows and yearlings. Bachelor bulls chase and indulge in mock battles with others of their kind, occasionally making forays into the breeding areas—only to be chased away by adult males. Such youthful

Bigger is better for adult male Steller sea lions, shown with females in the top photo, as well as for northern elephant seals (above).

behavior continues for several years, until a bachelor is capable of competing for a territory all his own.

Among otariids, most territorial boundaries follow natural lines, such as ridges in rock. "Actually, the bull's attachment may be stronger to this plot than to the 'wives' who share it with him," observed Victor Scheffer in his biography, *Adventures of a Zoologist.* "He may or may not—depending on his mood and her sexual condition—try to recapture a cow on the point of deserting his harem." Should a Steller sea lion bull become possessive, however, he can be brutal to his mates, blocking a departing female's way with his body or grasping an escapee in its jaws and throwing her back into his territory.

Bulls also try to steal mates away from each other, taking every opportunity to divide and conquer each other's holdings. So they won't waste time on nonbreeding activities, most bulls fast. They rely on stored fat, surviving for several weeks or, in the case of the Steller sea lion, for as long as three months without food or drink. Nonetheless, a Steller bull can muster the strength to issue as many as 400 warnings to other bulls, engage in a dozen battles and copulate with as many as 30 females during a single season at the rookery. By the time the last impregnable females have left the rookery, a steadfast bull may have lost almost a third of his adult weight, shedding more than 400 pounds.

A bull Steller sea lion's bulk helps it through the breeding season, providing fat reserves that can sustain it for three months. This male dwarfs the surrounding females.

A MOTHER'S WORK Female pinnipeds ordinarily don't defend territories, but their lives at the rookeries are just as taxing. Many Steller sea lion females are already pregnant when they arrive at the rookery, having carried their unborn pups for the previous months at sea. Research indicates that females frequently return to the same rookery site over successive years. In many instances, this site may be (the same or very close to) the place that the female was born.

Pregnant females give birth in a matter of days, usually to single pups and, in rare instances, twins. Because of the harsh marine environment, parenting among all marine mammals requires major investments of energy. For this reason, all marine mammal species give birth and rear one young at a time.

The newborns resemble wrinkled raisins, wrapped in dark brown to black fur and weighing 35 to 50 pounds. Within an hour of their arrival, most pinniped pups are ready to nurse. Nuzzling its mother's belly, a pup will latch onto a teat, greedily drinking its fill of nutritious milk. With a fat content of 20 to 55 percent, the milk of seals and seal lions is perhaps the richest of any mammal—considerably richer than that of human females. There's a good reason for this rich diet among otariids, whose pups are left on shore, often for as long as seven days, while their mother's search for food. Mother's milk must sustain them throughout this period of solitude. In many phocids, pups must fast for weeks or months after they are weaned. Their fat stores get them through this difficult time. In addition, pups born on ice must rapidly build up layers of blubber. A fat-rich diet is essential for blubber production. Broken down during digestion, blubber provides pinniped pups with metabolic water.

Drinking about two quarts of milk each day, a Steller sea lion

Pups, like this suckling northern elephant seal (below), grow quickly on fat-rich milk. A mother California sea lion cares for her pup (bottom) between bouts of feeding at sea.

pup can gain up to 12 ounces within 24 hours, doubling its weight in six to ten weeks. As the pup grows, it changes in other ways. It sheds its natal coat, replacing this pelage with thicker hairs of a lighter brown hue. In successive molts, each replacement hair will be lighter in color, eventually matching that of its parents.

During its first days in the rookery, Steller sea lion pups receive the highest degree of protection and care. Females fight for more room after the birth of their pups, snapping at any other females within reach. In some species, the older, more experienced females make the best mothers. This suggests that while some parenting skills are instinctual, others have to be learned.

A pup's chances of survival may depend in part on its sex. In Steller sea lions, as in many polygynous pinniped species, male pups weigh more at birth and may even receive more milk, enabling them to grow more quickly than females. Surprisingly, sex-linked survival factors sometimes cancel each other out: a study of Steller sea lion mothers and pups at California's Año Nuevo Point found that, while males spent more time suckling, their mothers were also gone for longer periods than the mothers of female pups.

With each week that passes, Steller sea lion pups receive less maternal care. A large percentage of pups—in some species as much as 40 percent—die in storms or accidents in or near the rookery. Many are unintentionally crushed by bulls who, in their zeal to defend territories or mate with females, may clamber over them. As if to avoid such a fate, young sea lions huddle at the sea's edge, wading in tide pools and sleeping away from their parents. Even here, the pups are not entirely safe. Crashing waves can sweep pups from rocky shorelines and into the water, drowning the inexperienced and easily fatigued swimmers.

As this harp seal pup grows, its pelage will change color, from pure white to black and white.

PLAYFUL PUPS Pups that survive these hazards develop quickly. By the time Steller sea lions are three months old, they will have moved out of their wading pools and into the shallow surge channels near shore. Both on land and in the water, pups play for many hours each day. They pair off, then lunge and parry with each other in mock combat, trying to nip their opponent without getting bitten in return. Or they may push at each other in contests of physical strength.

While pups may engage in some of this activity simply for fun, they may also be practicing for more serious adult roles—developing techniques for defending territories, avoiding predators or copulating. Playful exercises may continue throughout a pinniped's first years of life.

Researchers have watched young seals and seal lions playing catch with live prey. According to biologist Marianne Riedman, author of *The Pinnipeds: Seals, Sea Lions and Walruses*, games along the coast of Monterey, California, might include playing "Frisbee" with small ocean sunfish (*Mola mola*). Rocks, kelp, ice chunks and driftwood also become toys for some pups. Juvenile sea lions are particularly adept at underwater sports, spending hours romping, wrestling and racing with other youngsters beneath the waves.

Like many other otariids, Steller sea lion females often care for their pups as yearlings. Eyewitnesses in Alaska and British Columbia have even reported mothers nursing youngsters over three years of age. However, it's more typical for young Steller sea lions to continue nursing only until the next pup is born. Occasionally, juveniles and newborns will suckle side-by-side.

Galápagos sea lion pups refine their swimming skills in channels and pools (top), while young northern elephant seals (above) bask at the water's edge.

THE CYCLE CONTINUES Eleven days to two weeks after the delivery of their pup, Steller sea lion females are ready to mate. While many ice-breeding pinniped species copulate in the water, most land-breeding pinnipeds, including Steller sea lions, impregnate their mates on land. Observations of Steller sea lions reveal that females sometimes initiate copulation, directing their courtship behavior at the older, more proven bulls. The males of most pinniped species appear less picky about choosing mates. In their drive to impregnate every receptive female in the rookery, they sometimes injure their sex partners.

Although copulation can be rushed, the outcome of mating—a developing embryo—moves at a much slower pace. In Steller sea lions, the actual period of embryo growth is about eight months—a typical growth period for many mammals on land and at sea. Among Steller sea lions, the fertilized egg develops for a few weeks, then stops growing for about three months, after which it attaches to the uterine wall. Once attached, the embryo continues to grow.

Such delayed implantation is common among several other pinnipeds. While the cause of this delay is not known, its outcome is quite clear: it effectively sets the date of the pup's birth in the following year, when conditions will be favorable and the female makes her reappearance at the rookery. The length of delayed implantation may vary from two to five months, depending on the species of seal or sea lion.

At the end of the breeding season, Steller sea lion bulls and young bachelor males leave the rookery islands first, heading for other seasonal haunts. Females follow within one to two months,

Mating typically occurs on land for most pinnipeds, like these elephant seals (note the severe shark bite on the male's hind quarters) (top), often preceded by courtship at sea, as in the case of these playful California sea lions (above).

and pups leave last. Both sexes will congregate at a number of
different places, hauling themselves onto boulders, reefs, beaches,
and non-natural structures such as jetties and breakwaters, buoys,
and floating docks.

Sites used as rookeries in the breeding season also may be

used as haul-out sites during other times of year. Some mating may occur at these sites, usually between females that are not giving birth and males that cannot hold territories. Steller sea lions may also forego haul-out sites for long periods, choosing to rest on the water's surface in tightly packed groups called rafts.

Gregarious by nature, Steller sea lions even congregate offshore.

3

LIFE AT SEA

The rookeries of northern fur seals are just as crowded and action-packed as those of Steller sea lions. Adult males are the first to arrive at these remote Pribilof Island sites, a few weeks before the first pregnant females come ashore in June. The newly arrived females give birth within a day or two, then devote much of their time to rearing their young.

Such onshore devotion to the pups, however, is short-lived. By early August, nursing females will have returned to the ocean, pursuing squid and schooling fish roughly 100 miles, or as far as 260 miles, from land. Although the wide-ranging mothers return to the rookery at regular intervals to nurse, they are clearly more comfortable at sea. On average, females spend nearly three-fourths of the pup rearing season—approximately 90 of 125 days from birth to weaning—far away from dry land.

OCEANIC ANIMALS To both male and female northern fur seals, such a stint in the ocean could be considered brief. A typical year in the life of one of these ocean-going animals involves 300 to 330 days at sea. Young fur seals may spend even more time afloat. Once weaned, pups usually remain in the water until the next breeding season, taking their first, waddling steps on shore the following year. Unlike many other pinniped species (which come ashore to molt or rest), they come on land only to give birth and rear young.

While all pinnipeds, like this thermo-regulating California sea lion, are quite comfortable in water, the northern fur seal (right) spends most of its life at sea.

Through fall and winter and well into spring, northern fur seals swim, drift, dive and even sleep in the open ocean. "Its flippers are never dry in winter," wrote Victor Scheffer in *The Year of the Seal*. "The only solid thing they touch is the sleek body to which they are bound, and which they groom and scrub in endless play of motion."

Grooming is of paramount importance to northern fur seals. They rely on their coats as well as their blubber for surviving in cold ocean water. Made up of about 370,000 hair and fur fibers per square inch, their exceptionally dense coat insulates the seal's body from cold. It is so effective that, just like the species with thick blubber and thin coats, northern fur seals must actually vent excess body heat by waving their large, highly vascularized flippers in the breeze.

A Change of Coats Like other species of pinnipeds, fur seals shed and replace their fur coats once a year through a process called molting. For some species, like elephant seals and Hawaiian monk seals, molting involves sloughing off entire patches of hair and skin. The process takes one or two months, and the animals are more or less "grounded"—unable to leave the land—during this time. Some species, including the northern elephant seal, also fast during the molting process.

Coming ashore to molt, northern elephant seals often cover themselves with sand and gravel — a good way to keep cool despite the sun's warming rays.

Northern fur seals molt gradually, shedding fur over the course of a year. In this way, the seals can replace old hair and fur and still stay warm throughout the year. Molting has little effect on their swimming and feeding habits. A complete molt can take as long as three years.

MOVING WITH THE SEASON Besides molting, a second cyclical phenomenon directs the lives of many pinnipeds—the seasonal migration to and from feeding and breeding grounds. Fishes, birds, reptiles, insects and many other animals also migrate to feed and breed. Pinnipeds migrate to capitalize on seasonal abundance of food, to molt, and to seek nurturing environments for rearing their pups. While the migration distances of arctic species can be short, often following the annual movements of floating ice, some pinniped journeys cover many thousands of miles. Among pinnipeds, the record for such long-distance travel is held by female and juvenile northern fur seals, whose yearly round trips from rookeries in the Pribilof Islands in the eastern Bering Sea to winter hangouts along the southern California coast encompasses 6,000 miles.

Traveling at top speeds of four to five miles per hour, with frequent rest stops along the way, a female or juvenile northern fur seal may travel for several months to complete one leg of its trip. Females, juveniles and pups leave the rookeries by late November and migrate south, staying offshore until March, when they begin to return to the rookeries. Adult males leave the rookery grounds much earlier—from late August through October—but remain in the North Pacific and Bering Sea, returning to their rookeries in late May or early June.

Unlike northern fur seals, which migrate great distances, these southern fur seals stay close to their habitats near the South Georgia Islands.

No one really knows what initiates the pinnipeds' travels or how these animals are able to find their way, often across vast stretches of open ocean. Possible triggers include the lengthening or shortening of daylight hours, changes in water temperature and other environmental signals. A mature pinniped also may be receiving messages from its body—internal cues such as fluctuating levels of hormones governing breeding or other activities.

To find their way, migrating seals may depend on an array of navigational aids—the contours of the seafloor, the direction of the wind, the position of sun, moon and stars and possibly their "geographic memory"—an inborn recognition of the coastal

landscape—to guide them. Some scientists propose that the seal's eye is attuned to the turquoise color of coastal waters, making it easy for these animals to keep close to shore.

There's also evidence that magnetism may be leading the way. Several marine mammal species carry tiny particles of a black oxide of iron, called magnetite, in their heads. Like other iron oxides, magnetite particles are strongly affected by magnetic fields. It's possible that pinnipeds can use these particles to read the Earth's magnetic field like a map. Young seals can successfully wend their way north during their first migration, without parents or other seasoned travelers to guide them, suggesting that such map-reading ability may be innate.

Guided by subtle clues from their surroundings, many pinniped species routinely travel great distances.

SUITED FOR SUBMERSION

Many different adaptations—both anatomical and physiological—help deep-diving pinnipeds complete their difficult downward journeys. Without these, they could not endure near-freezing water temperatures and withstand great pressure—14.7 pounds per square inch for each 33 feet they descend.

Before making a deep dive, a pinniped expels air, emptying its lungs to reduce buoyancy and to prevent nitrogen gas from escaping from the lungs into the bloodstream. In humans, this causes a potentially fatal condition called "the bends."

The pinniped quickly closes its slit-like nostrils, and as the animal descends further, the pressure increases, causing its lungs to collapse. Any leftover air from the lungs goes to rigid spaces in the upper airways that are more able to withstand pressure.

As the pinniped glides quietly downward, its heart rate slows rapidly, decreasing from 120 beats per minute to four or six beats per minute over the course of the dive. The heartbeat of some species actually stops for ten seconds or more. The amount of blood leaving the heart is also severely reduced. Blood pressure is maintained by an enlargement in the main artery, which meters out blood even after the heart has stopped pumping.

Simultaneously, blood vessels constrict and certain muscles tighten, shutting off the blood supply to the viscera and reducing the flow to other parts of the body. In this way, the pinniped ensures that its two most crucial and easily damaged organs—its heart and brain—will be supplied with oxygen throughout the dive. Many species "borrow" oxygen from myoglobin, an iron-containing protein in muscles that, like the blood's hemoglobin, can store or release oxygen as needed. Stores of myoglobin in most pinnipeds are several times greater than those found in muscles of terrestrial mammals.

During particularly long dives, blood-deprived organs slow down or shut themselves off for a few minutes. As oxygen in the bloodstream is depleted, the muscles of many pinnipeds rely on anaerobic glycolysis—an energy-generating process for breaking down glycogen without consuming oxygen. However, this process is only an eighth as effective as glycolysis with

Highly specialized swimmers, pinnipeds can leisurely descend head-first, cruise beneath the waves, and spend time on the seafloor.

oxygen. It also produces a by-product, lactic acid, which builds up in body tissues and can ultimately cause organ damage. Rather than rely on this route, blood-deprived organs slow down or shut themselves off for a few minutes.

When the pinniped returns to the surface after a deep dive, it often takes a series of deep breaths, replenishing the blood's oxygen supply. In several species, the heartbeat also increases, vigorously pumping oxygen-rich blood to all parts of the body. After a surface interval—from several hours to a few minutes, depending on the species and the depth and duration of the dive—the animal is ready to plumb the depths once more.

Solitary Swimmers At sea, northern fur seals occasionally travel in pairs. For the most part, however, they are solitary swimmers, separated from other fur seals by as much as a square mile of ocean. Northern fur seals usually feed at night, when their prey—primarily small schooling fish and squid—rise from the depths after dark. Small fish, less than 10 inches long, are swallowed in a single gulp, whereas larger prey are brought to the surface, where they are broken into bite-sized chunks.

A harp seal feeds under the ice in Canada's Gulf of St. Lawrence.

Although northern fur seals can remain under water for up to seven minutes and dive as deep as 600 feet, studies conducted in the Bering Sea indicate that most dives are fairly short, lasting about a half to a third of this time. These short sojourns seldom take the seals more than 200 feet beneath the waves.

For many other pinnipeds, such a short dive would barely qualify as a dip. New Zealand sea lions (*Phocartos hookeri*), for instance, are known to dive to 1,320 feet in pursuit of prey, while Weddell seals can go even deeper, bottoming out at 1,980 feet. Such accomplishments are eclipsed by the northern elephant seal, which can descend to 4,125 feet—completing a round trip of a vertical mile and a half in 34 minutes. Only two other air-breathing animals—the sperm whale (*Physeter macrocephalus*) and the beluga whale (*Delphinapterus leucas*) are capable of making deeper dives.

The dives of northern elephant seals aren't just deep; they are nearly continuous. Most marine mammals perform a series of repetitive dives with intervals of swimming or resting at the surface in between these bouts. Northern elephant seals, however, seldom stay at the surface for more than a few minutes, taking extended, 20-minute breaks only on rare occasions. In one instance, researchers recorded the behavior of a female elephant seal for 34 days as she dove practically without pause, resting and swimming at the surface for no more than three minutes at a time.

DELVING INTO DIVING To record the dive patterns of northern elephant seals, researchers rely on the animals' seasonal cycles and capitalize on the latest technological advances. After nursing their pups, female elephant seals routinely go to sea, regaining the large amount of weight lost during the previous four weeks on land. But before they leave, researchers sedate some of the animals and glue a small epoxy cradle to the hair above their shoulders. The cradles are designed to hold an array of instruments the seals will carry with them on their dives—computerized time-depth recorders, thermometers, light sensors and swim-speed indicators. Each cradle also carries a tiny radio transmitter, which sends signals to a radio receiver on land.

Ten weeks later, when the females return to the same beaches, researchers trace the signals from the radio transmitters to locate their study animals. After sedating the females for a second time, they retrieve the instruments and the data. In another two weeks, the seals will begin to molt, sloughing off skin and hair—and the epoxy cradles.

These techniques for monitoring the elephant seal's progress under water have proved remarkably reliable: of the 26 recorders employed during the first five years of study, only five were lost at sea. Data from these studies have shown the most common depth preference is about 1,650 to 1,815 feet, reflecting the depths of prey items such as squid and fish.

Data also indicate that an elephant seal's daytime dives are approximately 330 feet deeper than its night dives. Researchers speculate that the seals may be feeding in the so-called deep scattering layer, populated by lanternfishes and hundreds of other light-producing marine species that rise to the surface at night and return to the depths by day.

Using other high-tech gear, researchers hope to gain more insights into diving behavior in future years. Teams of scientists intend to peer into the depths with miniaturized video cameras, and to identify the location of each seal (a process called global positioning) with more powerful signal transmitters carried by individual seals.

A researcher fastens an instrument pack on a 1,200-pound northern elephant seal (left). The pack on this female elephant seal (right) will fall off when the elephant seal molts.

PINNIPED PREDATORS

Because of their amphibious lifestyles, pinnipeds face more predators than do animals that dwell solely in water or on land. Carnivorous land mammals, birds of prey, sharks, and even other seals are just some of the animals that routinely feast on the flesh of seals and sea lions.

On land, pinnipeds are hunted by wolves, Arctic foxes, coyotes, eagles, and, in the Southern Hemisphere, pumas and hyenas. Basking on fast ice or pack ice, bearded seals, ringed seals and a few other Arctic seal species are also susceptible to sneak attacks by polar bears. While hunting seals on snow or ice, these all-white bears will hide their telltale black nose with their paw, according to Eskimos and a few non-native explorers.

At sea, some seals and sea lion species must be ever watchful for swift, carnivorous orcas, also called killer whales, which travel in extended family groups called "pods" and hunt as coordinated teams. Even the largest pinnipeds are open to attack from these sleek black-and-white mammals. "They acted like wolves on land," wrote one Russian biologist in the 1930s, describing the strategy of a killer whale pod for dispatching walruses.

They surrounded the group of walruses on all sides; then, six or seven on each flank formed straight lines, each whale just behind the head of the next; five approached the walruses from the front and ten came in from behind. Then one of the whales which had come in from the rear burst into the herd and divided it, whereupon the others moved into that location, and the water there boiled as in a caldron.

Walruses, southern sea lions and a few other seal and sea lion species are known to prey on pinnipeds. Perhaps the most voracious of these is the leopard seal, whose diet includes crabeater seals, southern elephant seals, and several other antarctic species. Leopard seals are said to eat anything that moves—including penguins, sea snakes, fish, squid and krill.

Large sharks also prey on pinnipeds in water. Seals and sea lions with open wounds and circular scars from the teeth of great white sharks are frequently seen at rookeries and haul-out sites in the Farallon Islands off San Francisco, near Dangerous Reef in South Australia, and at other locales. Remains of elephant seals and harbor seals are often taken from the stomachs of great white sharks captured or found dead along the California coast. It's thought that many shark attacks on people may be cases of mistaken identity, because from a shark's point of view, a human surfer on a short board may resemble a seal or sea lion.

Some scientists speculate that deep diving helps the northern elephant seal avoid shark attacks. They point out that animals swimming on or near the surface are silhouetted against the light, making them stand out to a shark patrolling the waters below. There have been no observations of white sharks below 300 feet, so by spending as much time below this depth, the seals can stay out of sight. Rarely do elephant seals swim at the surface or "porpoise" like sea lions, even while traveling to and from their rookeries.

Polar bears (below) stalk pinnipeds on ice, while orcas track down prey in the ocean, even nabbing an occasional sea lion in the surf zone off the Argentina coast (right).

4

PINNIPEDS AND PEOPLE

A small boat lies anchored in a quiet bay on the Washington coast. Its occupants, two commercial salmon fishermen, get ready to haul in their nets. But below the surface of the bay, several adult harbor seals are already enjoying the catch of the day. With their sharp teeth, the seals tug at the tails of the salmon, gobbling whatever fish they can tear free and taking chunks from the rest.

When the fishermen reel in their nets, they discover the remains of the seals' feast—several dozen salmon heads. Loudly cursing the seals, the pair vow never again to set their nets in this particular part of the bay.

URBAN OPPORTUNISTS Up to six feet in length and weighing from 70 to 300 pounds, harbor seals are common inhabitants of both Atlantic and Pacific coasts, as well as Europe and northern Asia. Some are gray, white or silver; others are black or dark brown, marked by light-colored rings or dappled with pale spots. The coats of some harbor seals may also be tinged with rust-colored or greenish hues, possibly from iron deposits and algae growing amid the fur.

Offshore, harbor seals travel singly, as mother-pup pairs or in small groups. They can sleep with their bodies nearly submerged in the water, exposing only the tip of their nose with its two v-shaped nostrils to the air—a posture commonly called bottling.

On land, harbor seals tend to congregate in smaller groups

Setting their gill nets in salmon-rich seas, commercial fishermen (below) often squabble with opportunistic harbor seals (right) over their share of the catch.

than most other pinniped species, with peak gatherings of more than 200 animals. Hauled out on beaches, boulders or break-waters, individuals typically assume arched positions.

Rocks are convenient perches for harbor seals, which prefer to forage near shore.

Near developed areas, many harbor seals show signs of wear and tear—scars from collisions with boats, scabby skin from swimming in polluted water and, occasionally, gunshot wounds from disgruntled mariners.

Preferring to stay close to shore, harbor seals forage for a variety of fish and invertebrates. Smaller prey are swallowed whole under water, with larger prey often gobbled at the surface. A list of items from a harbor seal's stomach reads like a seafood restaurant menu: flounder, herring, tomcod, hake, sculpins, pollock, shiner perch, cod, eelpout, salmon, rockfish, squid and octopi have all been found inside harbor seals from the Pacific Northwest.

The opportunistic feeding habits of harbor seals can get them in trouble with people, as revealed by a recent study conducted in Washington State. By interviewing commercial fishermen, researchers were able to estimate the predation rates—expressed as percentages of salmon catches—that could be attributed to harbor seals. In some areas, seals took as little as 1.5 percent of the day's salmon catch. In others, the take approached 40 percent.

Estimates may be on the low side, since figures were based on fishermen's records of salmon that were damaged but left dangling in their nets. Short of interviewing the harbor seals themselves, there was simply no way to include those fish that were actually removed and eaten before the fishermen could get their hands on them. With daily catches valued at one thousand dollars or more, it's not surprising that many salmon fishermen have feelings of ill will toward harbor seals.

WHERE SEALS GATHER . . .

California sea lions haul out by the hundreds on Pier 39's floating docks.

Seals and sea lions have been accused of an array of wrongs—including the reduction of migratory fish runs in the Pacific Northwest. Despite efforts by state wildlife agents to disperse them, California sea lions have been congregating at the entrance to Lake Washington in Seattle. Here they have been consuming large numbers of steelhead trout—as much as 62 percent of the fish that journey inland to spawn each winter. Captured and released as far away as the southern California coast, most of the sea lions have returned to the locks within days or weeks. Wildlife biologists are stymied.

California sea lions have become noisy nuisances at several locales along the Pacific coast. In the 1980s, the numbers of sea lions at Pier 39 in San Francisco's West Marina ranged from 10 to 50. Then, after a particularly plentiful herring season in the early part of 1990, the sea lion population grew from 50 to 300 individuals, mostly males. So far, there's been no indication that these raucous visitors intend to leave their new waterfront haunt. A similar assemblage has been observed in British Columbia, where more than 1,500 sea lions have staked their claim to log booms off the Vancouver Island community of Nanaimo.

Harbor seals have also drawn fire from coastal shellfish growers, who are quick to blame large local populations for recent shellfish bed closures. To resolve such complaints, a research team looked at water conditions near three seal haul-out sites in Washington. Large numbers of fecal coliform bacteria—microscopic organisms normally found in the intestines of seals and other warm-blooded animals—were discovered at all three locales. The bacteria are commonly used as indicators, alerting people to the possible presence of bacteria and viruses that are harmful to human health. Routinely, commercial shellfish operations are discontinued whenever high fecal coliform levels are found. "Continued increase of seal populations will only increase the potential for conflicts involving harbor seals and shellfish operations," the researchers' report cautioned.

INDIAN HARPOONING SEAL, LAPUSH, WASH.

HUNTED FOR THEIR FURS North America's first peoples hunted seals and sea lions for many thousands of years, obtaining an array of products on which their lives depended. Pinniped skin was used for boat coverings; flesh, blubber and organs were eaten, and bones were sharpened into harpoon points and utensils. Flippers were turned into boot soles, intestines into waterproof clothing, and stomach linings into food storage containers. To the Aleutian Islanders, even a seal's whiskers had a use—as hat decorations.

For Native Americans, hunting was often a cooperative venture, conducted by groups in large boats or fleets of kayaks. These vessels were outfitted with a seal hunter's tools: stone-tipped lances and harpoons for throwing, wooden clubs for subduing their catch and inflated sealskin buoys to slow a harpooned seals' progress or keep its carcass afloat.

Hunting expeditions at sea were as perilous as they were productive, according to Charles M. Scammon, a seasoned nineteenth-century sea captain and author of *The Marine Mammals of the Northwestern Coast of North America.* "When going in pursuit of seals," wrote Scammon, "three or four natives embark in a canoe at an early hour in the morning and usually return the following evening. . . . Frequently during the early part of the day, in the spring months, fresh winds come from the eastward, causing a rough, short sea in the whirling currents about the mouth of the strait. At such times, these seal-fishers, or hunters, squatting in their canoes—which have a skin buoy lashed

An Indian harpoons a seal in this undated photo (top).

Tlingit artists often carved war helmets for warriors in the likeness of a bull Steller sea lion head (above).

Reminders of past exploitation, bones litter remote beaches (right). The traditional harvest of northern fur seals by indigenous people continues today (inset).

on each side of the bow—present not only a comical but perilous appearance, they being continually drenched with salt water by the toppling seas, and the canoes making as great a diversity of bounds and plunges as do the seals themselves."

Native seal hunters also acted alone. In northern latitudes, seals were frequently captured with large nets made of seal-hide thong stretched beneath the ice. Lying nearby, the hunter would scratch the surface of the ice with a bone instrument carved to resemble a seal's flipper, complete with claws. An inquisitive seal attracted by the sound would become enmeshed in the net. Hunters in these frigid regions also would stake out a seal's breathing hole, waiting silently, in some instances for several hours, for the seal to return to the surface for a breath of air—and the opportunity to impale one of these valuable animals on the end of a harpoon.

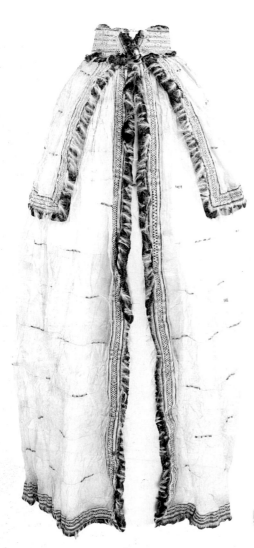

Aleutian Islanders made coats (left) and hats (below) from gutskin—processed sea lion intestine—that were both lightweight and waterproof. Lines made of seal hide were attached to these walrus- and seal-hunting harpoons (right).

POLLUTANTS LINKED TO DISEASE?

Fish that swim and feed in polluted seas often collect pollutants in their fat, which can eventually build up to higher levels than in their surroundings. Pinnipeds that eat these fish day after day can accumulate even higher pollutant levels. Chlorinated hydrocarbons, such as PCBs and DDT, are accumulated in the fat, while mercury, lead and other metals collect in the kidneys, liver, spleen and brain.

It's difficult to determine the effects of such accumulations. DDT and PCB contamination is thought to have caused numerous premature births among California sea lions on San Miguel and San Nicolas Islands, where pesticide concentrations were considerably higher in females and their dead premature pups than in the females that bore normal pups. Exceptionally high PCB levels have also been found in the fat of harbor seals that inhabit contaminated areas on Atlantic and Pacific coasts.

Pollution may have made European harbor seals more susceptible to a virus that, in the summer of 1988, led to the death of nearly 18,000 individuals off the coasts of Germany, Denmark, Great Britain and the Netherlands. Called phocine distemper virus, this disease weakened the immune system of seals, making them susceptible to other bacterial and viral infections. Most of the deaths occurred during the first two weeks of the outbreak.

Unusually warm weather and crowded conditions at seal haul-out sites may have combined to trigger the outbreak. As temperatures rose, seals began gathering in unusually dense herds on shore. Scientists theorize that, in such close quarters, the disease could spread quickly, like measles in a small schoolroom.

Weather and haul-out site conditions have not been conclusively linked to the spread of disease. However, four of the six documented mass mortalities among the world's seal populations have occurred in the past 20 years—a period that includes some of the warmest weather in the twentieth century. If pollution helped trigger the epidemic in the North Sea, then North American seals could be poised on the brink of a similar disaster.

Diseases can spread rapidly through crowded rookeries.

SLAUGHTERED AT SEA The tendency of pinnipeds to gather at predictable times and locations made them easy targets for exploitation by non-native people. The demand for seal pelts during the late eighteenth century inspired the wholesale slaughter of northern fur seals, primarily by Russian fur hunters who concentrated on the newly discovered rookeries in the Pribilof Islands. In 1789, the first shipment from the Pribilofs included the pelts of 2,000 sea otters and 40,000 fur seals. By 1803, takings had increased dramatically, with one commercial operation, the Russian American Company, shipping as many as 280,000 pelts to its headquarters in Siberia. Over the course of the firm's 20-year contract with Tsar Alexander I, about one million seal skins were exported.

By 1867, when the Russians sold Alaska and the Pribilof Islands to the United States, at least two and a half million pinnipeds had been slaughtered. An 1897 census showed fewer than 400,000 animals remained in the Pribilofs. After a massive public campaign to save the dwindling herd—backed by President Theodore Roosevelt and Dr. William Hornaday of the New York Zoological Society—the United States, Japan, Russia and Great Britain signed the North Pacific Fur Seal Convention of 1911, prohibiting the killing of seals for fur. The following year, the United States placed a five-year ban on all commercial seal hunting in the Pribilof Islands. Afterward, only young males could be harvested according to a strict quota system.

The quest for seal oil, considered a superior lubricant to whale oil, brought commercial harvesters from Russia, Europe and the United States to the rookeries of the northern elephant seal.

No longer over-harvested, populations of northern fur seals rebounded but are presently in decline due to fisheries interactions.

Populations were substantially reduced after a mere 50 years of hunting. "Owing to the continual pursuit of the animals, they have become nearly if not quite extinct on the California coast, or the few remaining have fled to some unknown point for security," wrote Charles Scammon in 1874. Today's northern elephant seals are descendants of those scant survivors—a single remnant population of less than 100 animals, discovered in 1909 on the western coast of Mexico's Baja California Peninsula. The seals' overlooked rookery, Guadalupe Island, is now a wildlife sanctuary, protected by the Mexican government.

Protected from hunters, northern elephant seals have been quick to rebound. Today, there are more than 125,000 of these once-beleaguered animals, with productive breeding colonies scattered from northern California to Mexico. The first pup born on the California mainland in this century was at Año Nuevo Point, part of Año Nuevo State Reserve, in 1975. Seventy miles north of Monterey and 40 miles south of San Francisco, Año Nuevo is the most accessible, hence the most popular, northern elephant seal rookery, attracting people from both urban centers and from throughout North America. Northern elephant seals come ashore at other mainland California locales: Cape St. Martin in Monterey County, Point St. George in Del Norte County and Point Reyes Peninsula in Marin County. However, the most densely populated breeding colonies are found in California's Channel Islands, where over half of the world population of northern elephant seals gathers each year. Other productive rookeries are on the Farallon Islands near San Francisco and on San Miguel and San Nicolas Islands near Los Angeles.

Guided tours of Año Nuevo's northern elephant seal rookery attract visitors during the fall and early winter breeding and pupping season.

PROTECTED BY LAW Killing continued well after many seal and sea lion stocks were seriously depleted. A series of misguided efforts to protect economically important stocks such as salmon, blackfish or cod led to outright warfare against harbor seals and their kin in the northwest. Singled out as threats to salmon resources, these animals were made victims of government-sanctioned extermination programs, with bounties—anywhere from $3 to $25 per seal—paid for each harbor seal pelt brought in. An estimated 200,000 to 240,000 harbor seals were killed in British Columbia between 1913 and 1969, while records from the Washington State Department of Fisheries for the years between 1947 and 1960 indicate that the bounty system ultimately led to the deaths of over 10,000 harbor seals. Oregon bounty hunters killed more than 500 seals each year between 1938 and 1942 along the Columbia River alone.

By the end of the nineteenth century, many pinniped species had all but vanished from many of their historic haunts. Recognizing that the wholesale slaughter of pinnipeds and other marine mammals could no longer continue unchecked, the United

These signs are reminders that seals and sea lions must be treated with respect.

States Congress passed the federal Marine Mammal Protection Act in 1972, making it illegal to harm or harass any of these animals in U.S. coastal waters. Primary responsibility for the protection of otariids and phocids was given to the Department of Commerce's National Marine Fisheries Service. A year later, the federal Endangered Species Act gave many pinniped species additional protection. Responsibility for managing walrus stocks in Alaska has passed several times between state and federal agencies and is currently with the U.S. Fish and Wildlife Service.

Even with legislative action, seals and sea lions have not been exempt from harassment. Until recently, provisions of the Marine Mammal Protection Act allowed the National Marine Fisheries Service to issue so-called "certificates of inclusion" to individual fishermen. Holders of these certificates could use firecrackers, slingshots, high-frequency acoustic devices and other equipment to legally harass seals and other marine mammals venturing too near their nets or other fishing gear. Certificate holders were also authorized to kill any animals actively preying upon their catch— but only as a last resort.

Although the commercial harvest of white-coated harp seals pups in the Gulf of St. Lawrence has stopped, the capture of as many as 10,000 harp seal pups by native peoples of Greenland and the Canadian Arctic is still permitted.

In 1994, this part of the Marine Mammal Protection Act was amended. Through a cooperative effort of fishermen's organizations and environmental groups, Congress developed a new package of rules to address accidental entanglements, harassment and lethal removal of marine mammals to protect fishing gear or catch. Commercial fishermen are no longer authorized to kill marine mammals during the course of their fishery. They can, however, continue to take actions to deter marine mammals "from damaging property or endangering personal safety." Depending on the likelihood of such encounters, individual fishermen may be required to keep detailed logbooks or carry on-board observers.

Also enacted in 1994, a new provision of the Marine Mammal Protection Act enables individual state governments to apply for authorization to intentionally kill pinnipeds in certain instances. Such authorization will not be granted if the pinniped stock is designated as depleted or listed as threatened or endangered under the Endangered Species Act. A special task force will be convened if a state can demonstrate that individually identifiable pinnipeds are causing harm to any salmon or steelhead stock that is listed as endangered or threatened or that migrates through into Lake Washington in Seattle (see *Where Seals Gather . . .* on page 51 of this book). After reviewing the evidence and considering public comment, this task force can recommend that the pinnipeds be killed. Further studies have been ordered to determine the effects of California sea lions and harbor seals, not only on salmon and steelhead stocks, but on aquaculture resources in the Gulf of Maine and the coastal ecosystems of Washington, Oregon and California.

PINNIPED PERILS Though protected by law in North American waters, seals and sea lions still face numerous threats. Each year, thousands become entangled in active, lost or discarded fishing nets. Unable to reach the surface for air, these victims of "ghost nets" soon suffocate and die. Off the California coast, it's been

Ensnared in marine debris, this young elephant seal could suffocate or die of hunger and thirst. Public and privately sponsored beach cleanups can help clear such life-threatening debris from the pinnipeds' path.

estimated that as many as 2,000 harbor seals—including what could amount to as many as five percent of California's harbor seal populations—were accidentally killed in this manner each year. Efforts to relocate such net fishing activities farther from shore have greatly reduced incidental catches of harbor seals in California.

Oil spills have also been blamed for the deaths of seals and sea lions. Because the insulating properties of a fur seal's coat can be severely hampered by oil contamination, these animals are among the more vulnerable to incidents such as the 1989 *Exxon Valdez* spill in Alaska's Prince William Sound. An even bigger health threat is posed to pinnipeds that inhale or absorb toxic hydro-carbons from oil. Detergents that are commonly used to disperse spilled oil along the coasts are believed to be equally hazardous to pinniped health.

For seals and sea lions, the steady development of our coastlines has meant the loss of access to historic haul-out areas. Especially hard hit have been harbor seals, which traditionally feed, breed and rear their young near shore. When the numbers of joggers, bicyclists and beach strollers reach a peak, the harbor seals begin looking for new places to haul out. Or they may modify their behavior, coming ashore after dusk or before dawn. Continued disturbance can lead to reduced pupping rates or abandonment of preferred pupping grounds.

California sea lions have learned to coexist with people (below). The presence of too many people, however, can cause problems for some species, including these harbor seals (bottom).

Under normal conditions, harbor seal pups are left on the beach for several hours while their mothers go fishing. People often think these wide-eyed animals are lost or abandoned. By removing them from beaches and bringing them to aquariums, zoos or animal shelters, they are actually causing problems for the young seals.

Several organizations work hard to undo the harm to pinnipeds from human activity. Reports of injured or abandoned pinnipeds are now channeled through a network of veterinarians and volunteers in Boston, Miami, Seattle and other coastal cities. If necessary, injured animals can be nursed back to health at public aquariums, marine laboratories or zoos. Workers with non-profit groups such as the Marine Mammal Center in Sausalito or the Friends of the Sea Lion in Laguna Beach, California, are equally active in coming to the aid of pinnipeds. Each year, specially trained crews at these facilities rescue hundreds of wounded or weakened animals, eventually releasing their healthy patients back to the sea.

A BRIGHTER FUTURE The steady build-up of many pinniped populations is a good sign that protective measures are working. The return of several once endangered species, including the northern elephant seal, is giving us a second chance to appreciate these animals in their natural settings. As this century draws to a close, we are in a better position to observe seals and sea lions than ever before.

We still have much to learn about these "feather-footed" beings, the pinnipeds. With our help, these facile swimmers will continue to grace our shores for many centuries to come.

Programs to protect the Hawaiian monk seal, like this mother and pup in the surf, are trying to reverse this animal's course toward extinction.

SEALS AND SEA LIONS FAMILY TREE

The Phocids

I. Subfamily Monachinae
  A. Elephant seals
    1. Southern elephant seal
      (*Mirounga leonina*)
    2. Northern elephant seal
      (*M. angustirostris*)
  B. Monk seals
    1. Hawaiian monk seal*
      (*Monachus schauinslandi*)
    2. Mediterranean monk seal*
      (*M. monachus*)
  C. Antarctic seals
    1. Weddell seal
      (*Leptonychotes weddelli*)
    2. Ross seal
      (*Ommatophoca rossi*)
    3. Crabeater seal
      (*Lobodon carcinophagus*)
    4. Leopard seal
      (*Hydrurga leptonyx*)

II. Subfamily Phocinae
  A. Hooded seal (*Cystophora cristata*)
  B. Bearded seal (*Erignathus barbatus*)
  C. Largha seal (*Phoca largha*)
  D. Ringed seal (*P. hispida*)
  E. Caspian seal (*P. caspica*)*
  F. Baikal seal (*P. sibirica*)
  G. Harp seal (*P. groenlandica*)
  H. Ribbon seal (*P. fasciata*)
  I. Harbor seal (*P. vitulina*)
  J. Grey seal (*Halichoerus grypus*)

The Otariids

I. Subfamily Arctocephalinae
  (Fur seals)
  A. Guadalupe fur seal
    (*Arctocephalus townsendi*)
  B. Juan Fernández fur seal*
    (*A. philippii*)
  C. Galápagos fur seal*
    (*A. galapagoensis*)
  D. South American fur seal
    (*A. australis*)
  E. New Zealand fur seal
    (*A. forsteri*)
  F. Antarctic fur seal
    (*A. gazella*)
  G. Subantarctic fur seal
    (*A. tropicalis*)
  H. Cape fur seal
    (*A. pusillus*)
  I. Northern fur seal
    (*Callorhinus ursinus*)

II. Subfamily Otariinae (Sea lions)
  1. New Zealand sea lion*
    (*Phocartos hookeri*)
  2. Australian sea lion
    (*Neophoca cinerea*)
  3. Southern sea lion
    (*Otaria byronia*)
  4. California sea lion
    (*Zalophus californianus*)
  5. Steller sea lion*
    (*Eumetopias jubatus*)

The Odobenidae (Walruses)

I. Walrus (*Odobenus rosmarus*)

*Endangered, threatened or vulnerable species from IUCN/SSC list.

INDEX